Content

I Saw Three Ships

Angels We Have Heard on High

O Come All Ye Faithful

O Come, O Come Emmanuel

O Little Town of Bethlehem

Once in Royal David's City

The First Noel

The Holly and the Ivy

The Twelve Days of Christmas

Toyland

Up on the House Top

We Three Kings

What Child Is This

While Shepherds Watched Their Flocks by Night

4) Write Your Own Composition!

How to Play Piano
(A Crash Course For Complete Beginners)

First, let's take a look at the piano. Go ahead, play some keys. What do you notice?

Some keys are low like elephants stomping around.

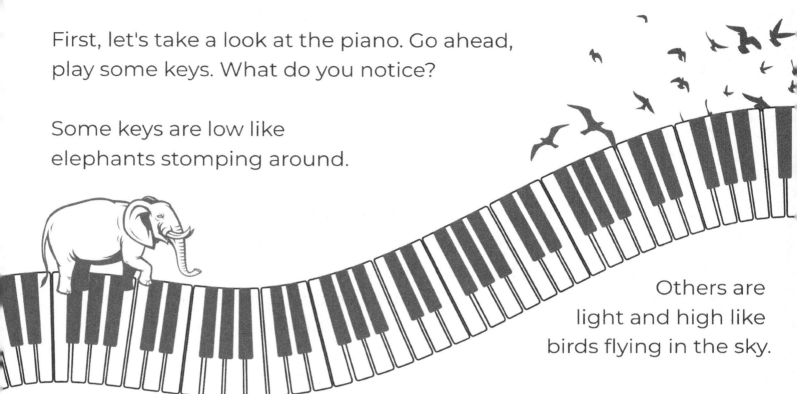

Others are light and high like birds flying in the sky.

Musicians write and read music in very much the same way as books. The lowest notes go at the very bottom, and the highest at the very top. Here are all the white notes, from the lowest (like the heavy elephant) to the highest (like the delicate bird).

The black dots (the **notes**) tell us what to play - whether it's high or low, fast or slow. They all hang from 5 lines like a washing line.

Those five lines are called the **staff.**

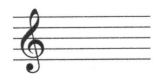 At the beginning of every new line there's a beautiful spiral shape called the **treble clef**.

All the black notes are called **sharps.** They sound a bit strange, a bit sharp to our ears perhaps. When writing music we write sharps with a **#** sign next to them.

After the treble clef comes the **time signature**. Every piece of music has a beat, a rythm, that you tap your foot along to. The time signature has two numbers - the number at the top tells us how many beats will be in each bar and the bottom number tells us which kind of note we will be tapping our feet along to.

4/4	3/4	6/8	3/8
4 beats of 4th notes	3 beats of 4th notes	6 beats of 8th notes	3 beats of 8th notes

Enough about notation, how do you actually play on a piano?!

Ok, ok. Let's have a look at the piano. We already figured out that there's white and black notes, but look even closer. What pattern can you see?

That's right! It's the same pattern again and again. 3 black keys, 2 black keys... again and again. These keys each have letters which are repeated along the entire length of the piano, called **octaves.**

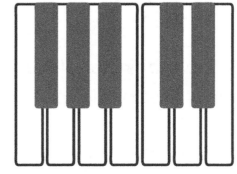

So what are these notes?

Well let's start with the easiest ones to remember.

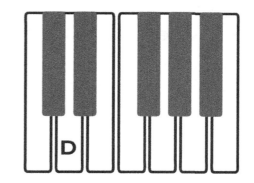

Find any two black keys. Notice how they look like two long ears of a dog? The note inbetween them is called the **D.**

Next, find the 3 black notes. Put your finger on the one in the middle then slip it to the next white note higher up the piano. This is the first note of the alphabet - the **A.**

Guess what? The rest of the notes follow the alphabet, so **B** comes after **A**, **C** after **B**, and back to the **D.** Now we can fill in all the letters, all the way up to **G**.

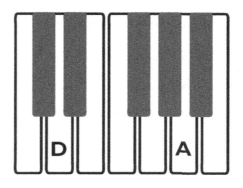

The sharps use the same letter as the white note to the left of them. So they look like this:

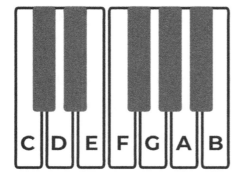

And voila! That's every single note on the piano!

The Notes

So now we know which notes to play, but for how long? Should they be quick and fast or long and slow? The type of note tells us how many beats to hold the key down for.

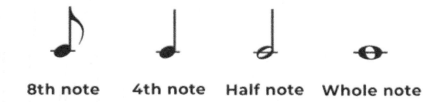

8th note   4th note   Half note   Whole note

A whole note is held down for twice as long as a half note, which is also the same as playing 4 quarter notes, or 8 eighth notes.

Sometimes we don't want to play anything! For these notes we rest and don't push any keys. In this book we will only use the quarter rest:

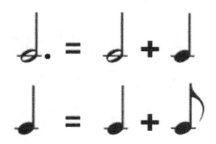

Dotted Notes

A dot after a note means that you should add half of the note to the note. So a dotted half note becomes a half + a quarter, and a dotted quarter becomes a quarter + an 8th.

The Repetitions

Sometimes we want to repeat certain parts of a song. Let's have a look at how we repeat different parts in piano sheet music.

Whenever you see these signs:

Repetition begins  **Repetition ends**

You can repeat everything within those brackets once. Like this:

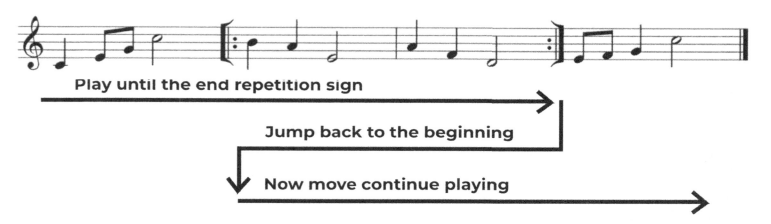

Sometimes there's multiple parts to play, first to play one section and then the next section. In music notation these sections are labelled with 1 and 2 to tell you which parts to play first (first 1, then 2). Like this:

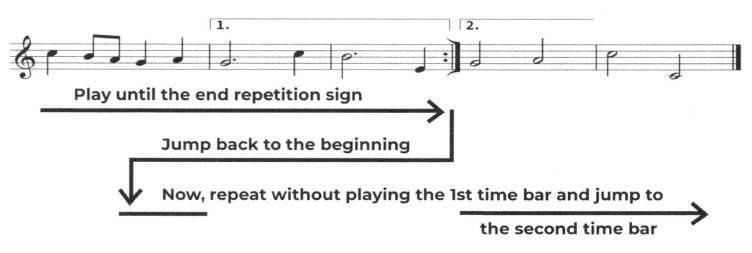

The Ties

In some songs you'll see some curved lines connecting notes together. They look a bit like skipping ropes or someone throwing a ball. They can also connect notes together across bars (over the fence). So when you see this symbol you should hold the key down until the second note is also finished - we add them together.

These tied 8th notes   These tied half notes   Ties can also work through bars.
now last 2 beats   now last 4 beats   The half note last 3 beats now

And that's it! Now you know everything you need to read and play every song in this book.

The MP3 Files

Good news! For every song in this book we have given you the additional MP3 file so you can listen along and hear exactly how it is played on piano. We recommend listening to each song first to get an idea of the exact rythm and how it is played on piano.

To access all the audio files you can scan this QR code on your phone, or follow the link below. The files will be shared with you through GoogleDrive.

shorturl.at/ntyS2

If you have any questions at all, feel free to contact us through email:
contactmontywebb@gmail.com

Away in a Manger

Jingle Bells

Silent Night

We Wish You a Merry Christmas

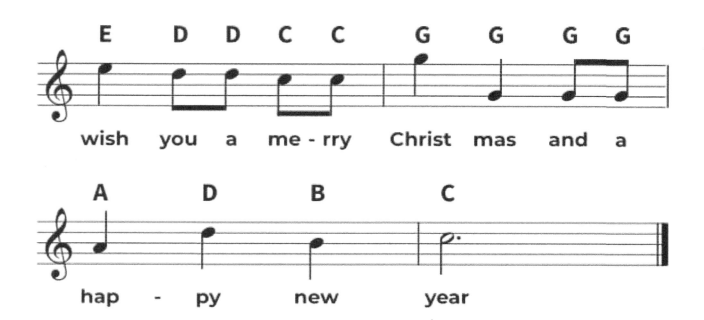

Angels From The Realms Of Glory

Joy To The World

sing And _ Hea - ven and na - ture _

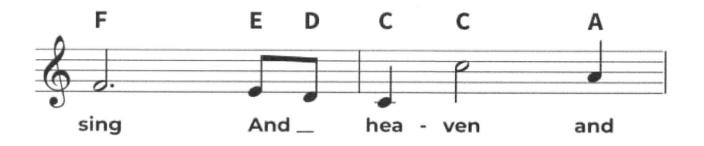

sing And __ hea - ven and

hea ____ ven and na - ture sing

(Joy To The World - page 2)

O Christmas Tree

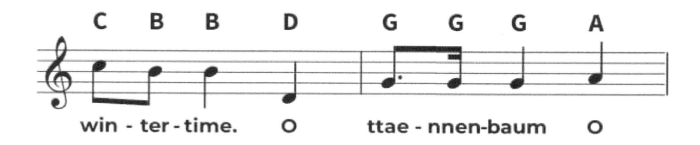

win - ter - time. O ttae - nnen-baum O

Christ-mas tree How love-ly are thy bran-ches!

(Oh Christmas Tree - page 2)

Auld Lang Syne

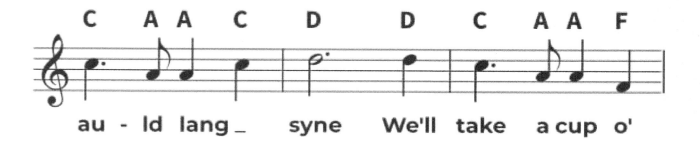

au - ld lang _ syne   We'll   take   a cup o'

kind-ness yet For _ days of auld lang syne

Coventry Carol

Deck The Halls

(Deck The Halls - page 2)

Go Tell It On The Mountain

(Go Tell It On The Mountain - page 2)

God Rest Ye Merry Gentlemen

E D C♯ B A C♯ B A D C♯ D

com _ fort and joy com-fort and joy Oh _

E D C♯ B A C♯ B A D C♯ D

com _ fort and joy com-fort and joy Oh _

Good King Wenceslas

Hark! The Herald Angels Sing

(Hark! The Herald Angels Sing - page 2)

Here We Come A-Caroling

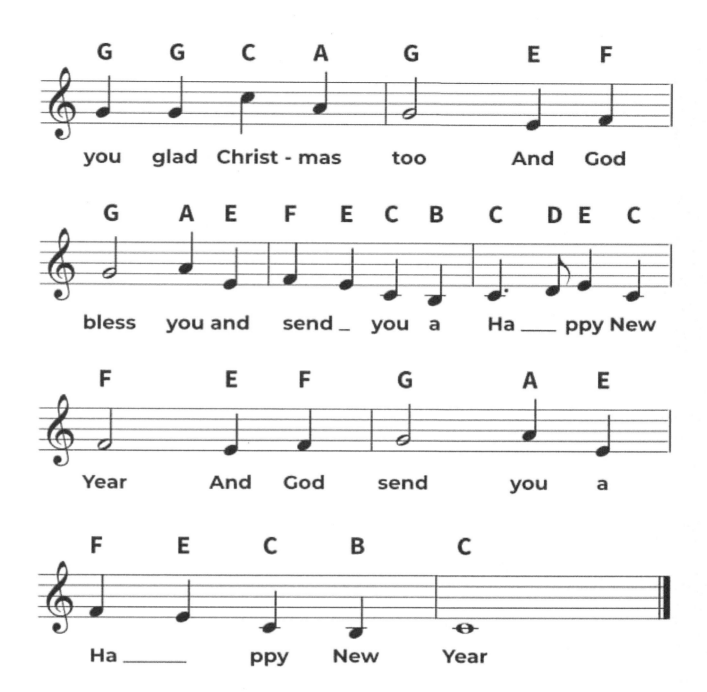

(Here We Come A-Caroling - page 2)

I Heard the Bells on Christmas Day

I Saw Three Ships

Angels We Have Heard on High

O Come All Ye Faithful

(O Come All Ye Faithful - page 2)

O Come, O Come, Emmanuel

O Little Town Of Bethlehem

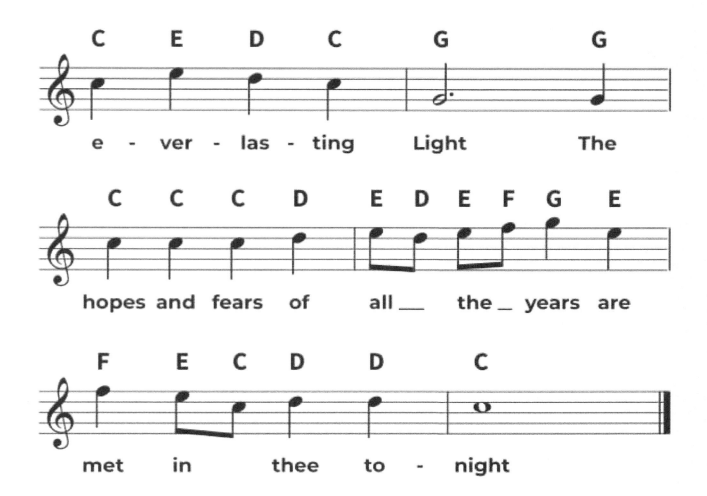

(Oh Little Town of Bethlehem - page 2)

Once in Royal David's City

The First Noel

The Holly and the Ivy

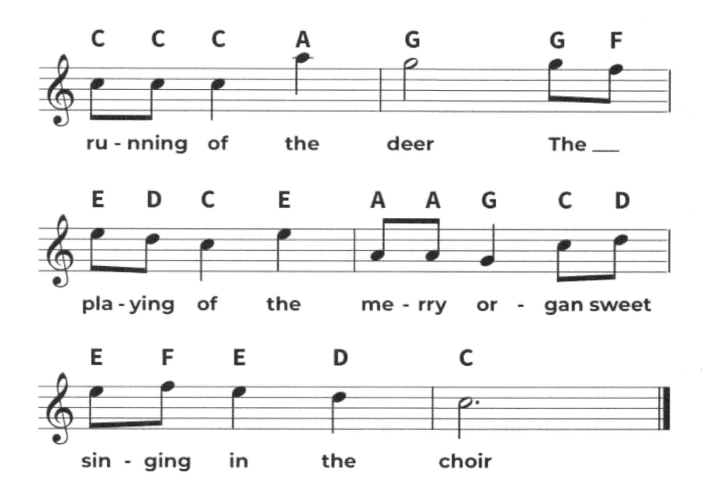

C C C A G G F
ru - nning of the deer The __
E D C E A A G C D
pla - ying of the me - rry or - gan sweet
E F E D C
sin - ging in the choir

The Twelve Days of Christmas

Toyland

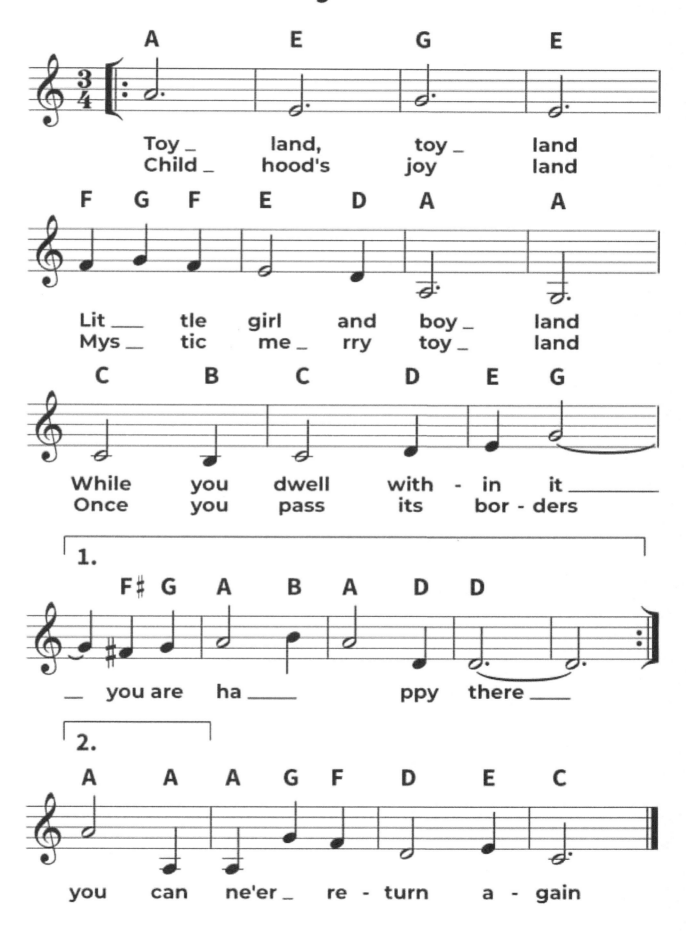

Up on the House Top

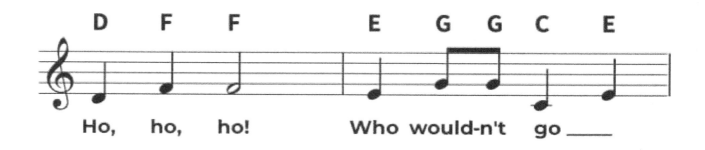

Ho, ho, ho! Who would-n't go ____

Up   on the house - top   click, click, click!

Down to the chim-ney with   good Saint Nick

(Up on the House Top - page 2)

We Three Kings

(We Three Kings - page 2)

What Child is This

(What Child is This - page 2)

While Shepherds Watched Their Flocks By Night

Write your own composition!

If you enjoyed this book please consider leaving us a **review on Amazon**. Leaving a review is the best thing you can do to support us - plus we just love reading your comments!

Other books by Monty Webb:

Made in the USA
Monee, IL
02 December 2024

72037456R00063